You and Your Pet
Hamster
and Gerbil

Jean Coppendale

QEB Publishing

Published in the United States by
QEB Publishing, Inc.
23062 La Cadena Drive
Laguna Hills
Irvine
CA 92653

Library of Congress Control Number 2004101777

ISBN 1 59566 055 0

Written by Jean Coppendale
Consultant Michaela Miller
Designed by Susi Martin
Editor Gill Munton
All photographs by Jane Burton except
page 20 (vegetables) by Chris Taylor
With many thanks to Adelle Tracey and Jumaane Bant
Picture of Cuddles on page 29 by Adelle Tracy

Creative Director Louise Morley
Editorial Manager Jean Coppendale

Printed and bound in China

Words in **bold**
are explained on
page 32.

Contents

Your first hamster or gerbil   4
Which pet?   6
Lots of pets   8
Pet shopping list   10
Getting ready   12
Saying hello   14
Handle with care   16
Feeding your pet   18
Keep it clean   20
Your gerbil's life cycle   22
Let's play!   24
Make a playground   26
Saying goodbye   28
Pet checklist   30
Parents' checklist   31
Pet words   32
Index   32

Your first hamster or gerbil

Hamsters and gerbils are lively little animals, and they love to play. Hamsters are nocturnal. This means that they like to sleep during the day and wake up at night.

▼ **Hamsters and gerbils are small and fragile.**

Hamsters and gerbils are very small and can easily get hurt. You should always handle them gently.

Parent Points

Hamsters are nocturnal, and so do not make good pets for young children because they tend to be asleep when the child wants to play. Hamsters and gerbils can easily get hurt if they are dropped, so they might not be appropriate pets for boisterous children. Children should always be supervised by an adult when they are playing with their hamster or gerbil.

Taking care of an animal is your responsibility, not your child's. Try to make sure that he or she is not going to get bored with the hamster or gerbil before you buy one.

▲ **Hamsters and gerbils usually live for between two to three years.**

Which pet?

Gerbils are
very active and
do not like to be
alone. It is best
to buy two brothers
or two sisters and keep
them together.

▲ Hamsters like to live alone.

Hamsters sleep during the day and wake up at night, so you will not be able to play with your hamster in the daytime.

▼ Do not mix gerbils and hamsters together.

Lots of pets

There are many different **breeds** of hamster and gerbil. They have different colored fur and different markings.

◄ **Black Mongolian gerbil**

► **Agouti Syrian hamster**

▼ **Lilac Mongolian gerbil**

◀ **Black Syrian hamster**

▲ **Golden satin Syrian hamster**

▶ **Albino gerbils**

Pet shopping list

Your hamster or gerbils will need:

Shredded white paper towels and a small cardboard box. Never use newspaper.

Or you could use hay...

...or wood shavings. Never use cedar or pine.

A cage or a plastic tank

▶ **Hamster food or gerbil food**

▲ **A scoop for cleaning out the tank**

◀ **A food bowl and a water bottle with a metal spout**

Your pet will enjoy some toys

Getting ready

The best home for a hamster or some gerbils is a plastic tank or a wire cage with a solid floor. It should be big enough for your pet to run around in.

Cover the floor with a layer of wood shavings. Add little piles of hay or shredded white paper towel so that your pet can make a cozy nest.

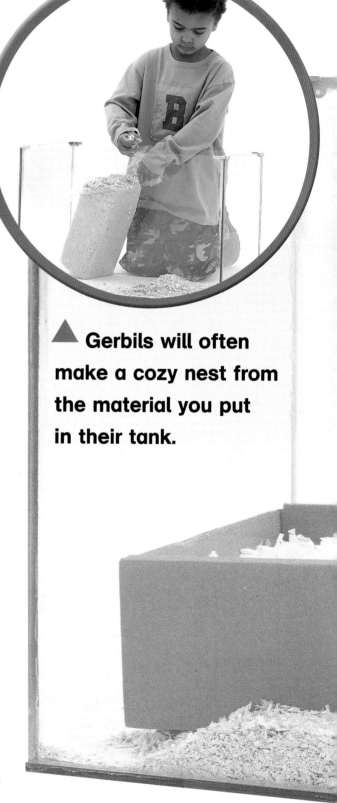

▲ **Gerbils will often make a cozy nest from the material you put in their tank.**

▲ **Make sure your hamster's tank or cage has a separate cozy nest box.**

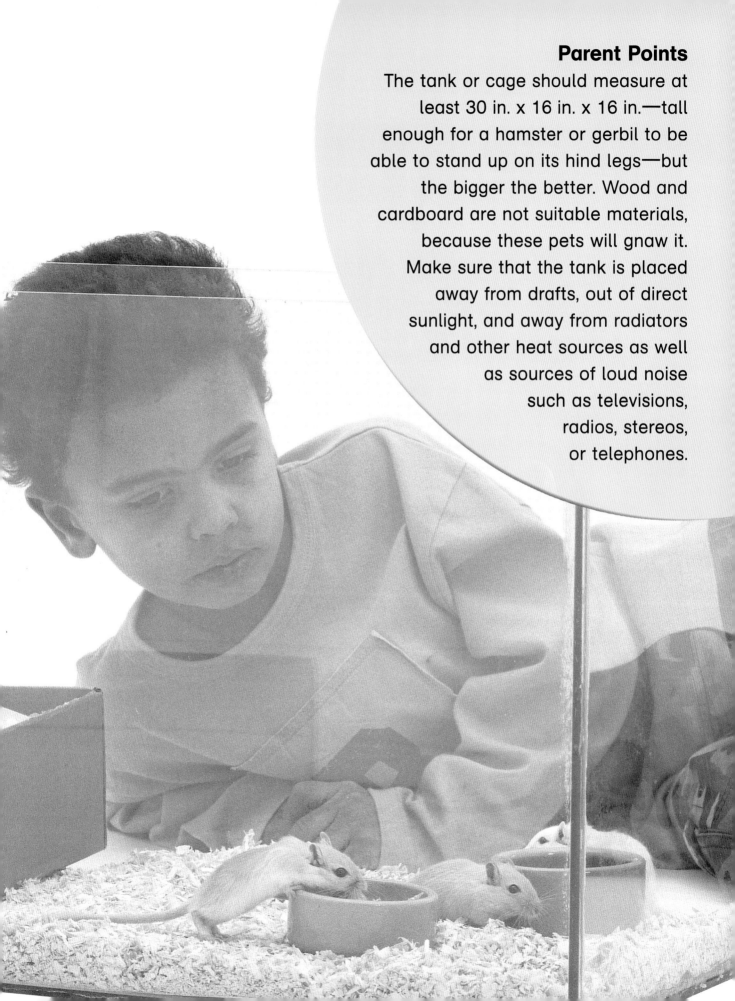

Parent Points

The tank or cage should measure at least 30 in. x 16 in. x 16 in.—tall enough for a hamster or gerbil to be able to stand up on its hind legs—but the bigger the better. Wood and cardboard are not suitable materials, because these pets will gnaw it. Make sure that the tank is placed away from drafts, out of direct sunlight, and away from radiators and other heat sources as well as sources of loud noise such as televisions, radios, stereos, or telephones.

Saying hello

When your pet first comes to live at your house, it might feel very scared. Place it gently in its tank or cage, and leave it alone for a couple of hours to get used to its new home.

Do not make any loud noises near it. Talk to it quietly, so that it gets to know your voice.

Do not make any loud noises or sudden movements near your pet.

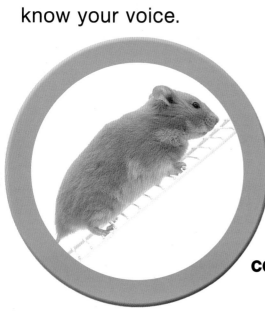

Soon, your pet will start to explore its new home and will enjoy running up and down ladders in its cage or tank.

Offer your pet a treat, such as a piece of apple. After a couple of days, your pet will start to get used to you and will let you cup it in your hand.

Parent Points
Make sure your child knows how to handle the hamster or gerbil before he or she tries to pick it up (see pages 16–17).

Handle with care

Hamsters and gerbils are very small, and a hand swooping down would scare them. Slowly put your closed hand into the tank or cage, and let your pet sniff it. Slowly open your hand, and let your pet climb onto your palm.

▲ **Always use two hands to hold your pet.**

◀ **To pick up your pet, gently scoop it into your palm. Never grab your pet around its body or dangle it by its tail.**

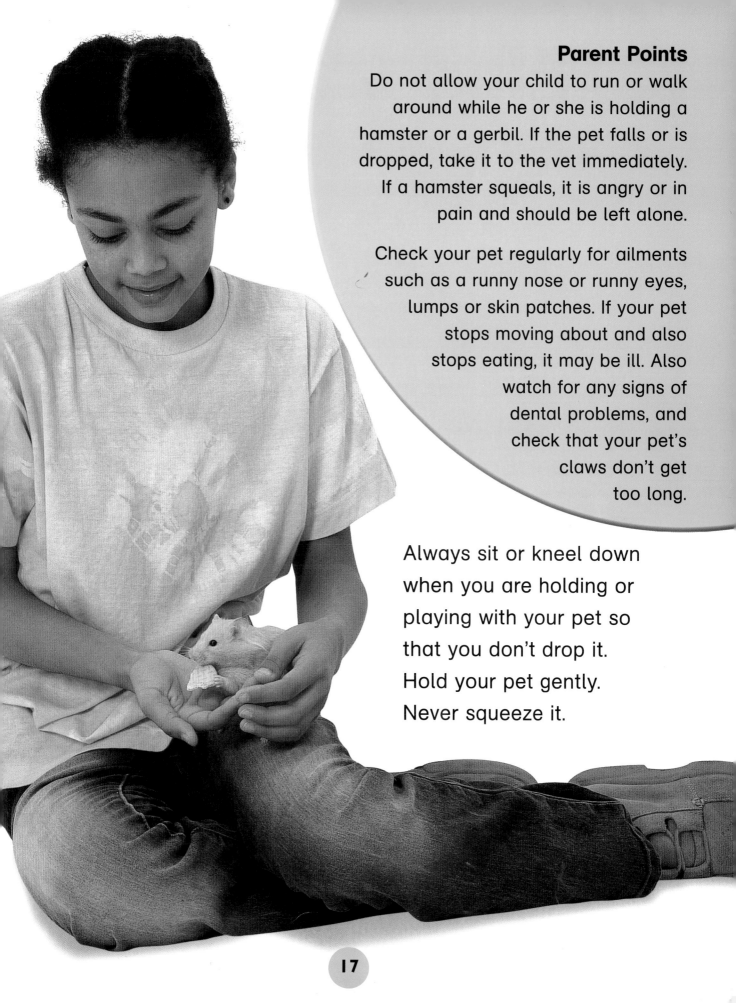

Do not allow your child to run or walk around while he or she is holding a hamster or a gerbil. If the pet falls or is dropped, take it to the vet immediately. If a hamster squeals, it is angry or in pain and should be left alone.

Check your pet regularly for ailments such as a runny nose or runny eyes, lumps or skin patches. If your pet stops moving about and also stops eating, it may be ill. Also watch for any signs of dental problems, and check that your pet's claws don't get too long.

Always sit or kneel down when you are holding or playing with your pet so that you don't drop it. Hold your pet gently. Never squeeze it.

Feeding your pet

Your pet should always have some food. Buy special hamster or gerbil food from a pet store or vet.

Carrot-shaped wood chew block

Feed your pet a piece of fresh fruit or vegetable every day. Try carrot, apple, celery, broccoli, banana, or cucumber.

As a treat, hide a piece of a plain cracker or dry bread in the cage for your pet to find. Never give it candy or sticky food.

Broccoli

Celery

Make sure your pet has a block of wood to gnaw on. This will help to keep its teeth short and healthy.

Make sure your pet's water bottle always has plenty of clean water in it.

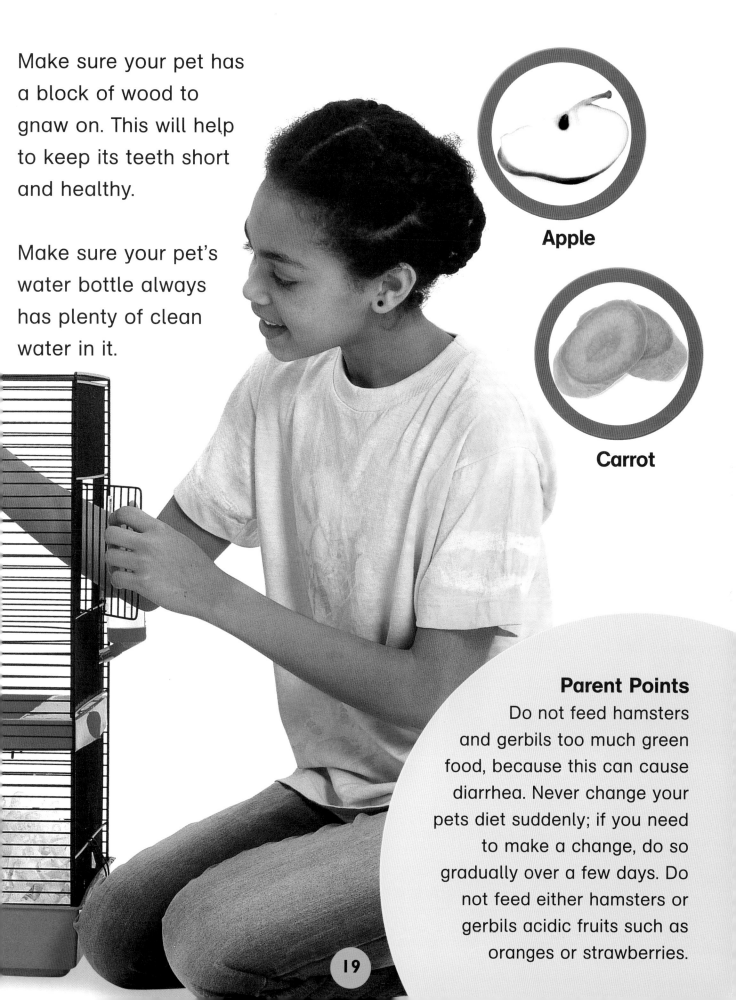

Apple

Carrot

Parent Points

Do not feed hamsters and gerbils too much green food, because this can cause diarrhea. Never change your pets diet suddenly; if you need to make a change, do so gradually over a few days. Do not feed either hamsters or gerbils acidic fruits such as oranges or strawberries.

Keep it clean

Your hamster's and gerbils' tank or cage needs to be kept clean. Once a day, use the scoop to clear out droppings and old bits of food.

Give the tank or cage a really good clean with a little animal-safe disinfectant. Wipe all the surfaces, and wash the toys.

Give your hamster's home a really good clean every week. You should clean out your gerbil's home every two weeks.

Wash the food bowl every day. Clean out the water bottle with a bottle brush once a week.

Always wash your hands when you are done cleaning out the tank.

Parent Points
Use animal-safe disinfectant (available from pet stores) for cleaning the tank. Make sure the pet is put somewhere safe while its home is being cleaned.

Your gerbil's life cycle

5

▶ When a female gerbil is about three months old, she can have babies. Her babies drink her milk. This is called suckling.

◀ At six weeks old, a gerbil is old enough to leave its mother.

4

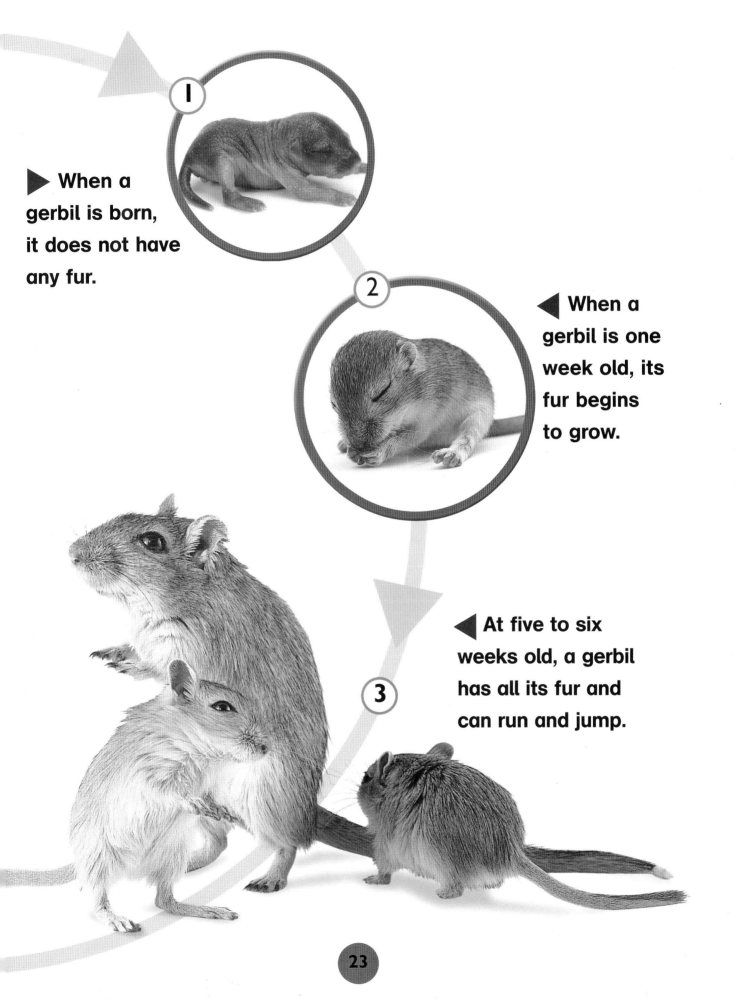

▶ When a gerbil is born, it does not have any fur.

1

2

◀ When a gerbil is one week old, its fur begins to grow.

◀ At five to six weeks old, a gerbil has all its fur and can run and jump.

3

Let's play!

Gerbils and hamsters are very active, so give your pet some toys. Put some cardboard tubes in the tank or cage. Cut holes in a plastic bottle for your pet to explore.

Hide food for your pet to find.

▼ **Your pet will love to climb in and out of holes.**

▶ As a treat, buy your pet a special habitat. You'll enjoy watching it have fun.

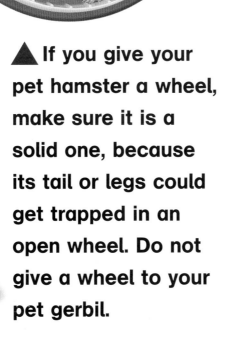

▲ If you give your pet hamster a wheel, make sure it is a solid one, because its tail or legs could get trapped in an open wheel. Do not give a wheel to your pet gerbil.

Parent Points
Hamsters and gerbils should be allowed out of the tank or cage once a day, so that they can get some exercise. Make a playground in a large cardboard box with some toys. Make sure your pet cannot escape into corners, under doors, up fire places, behind base boards, or into pieces of furniture. Keep cats and dogs out of the room.

Make a

Make a playground for your pet to exercise in. Use an old cardboard box, old toilet paper tubes, old paper towel tubes, and some cartons.

COMBI TV/VCR

OMBI TV/VCR

playground

Saying goodbye

Pets get older, just as people do. As your pet grows older, it will play less and spend more time sleeping. Don't give it as much food as before, or it will get fat.

My pet Cuddles

◀ **If your pet is ill, or appears to be in pain, take it to the veterinarian.**

If your child's pet dies, let him or her cry and express sadness. Writing a story about the pet—or putting together a scrapbook or montage of photos and drawings —can be very healing.

It is not always a good idea to replace the pet immediately—let your child grieve first.

Cuddles last summer

Keep a special scrapbook about your pet

If your pet is very old or ill, it may die. Try not to be too sad, and remember all the fun you had.

You may want to bury your pet in the yard, or you can take it to the veterinarian.

Pet checklist

Read this list, and think about all the points.

✔ **Hamsters and gerbils are not toys.**

✔ **Treat your pet gently —as you would like to be treated yourself.**

✔ **Gerbils and hamsters are very small and can easily get hurt if you are not gentle.**

✔ **How will you treat your pet if it makes you angry?**

✔ **Never shout at your pet, or frighten it.**

✔ **Animals can feel pain, just as you do.**

✔ **Will you be happy to clean out your pet's cage or tank every day?**

Parents' checklist

- **You**, not your child, are responsible for the care of the pet.

- Your pet will need someone to look after it every day when you are away from home—this includes feeding, cleaning, and exercising.

- Hamsters and gerbils are small pets, and can easily get stepped on—make sure your child is aware of the dangers.

- Exercise wheels are not appropriate toys for gerbils as their tails can become trapped.

- Hamsters will bite if they are scared or angry.

- Hamsters should be left to sleep during the day. Don't keep two hamsters together, even if they are from the same litter.

- Never use newspaper in your pet's cage—it is poisonous to both hamsters and gerbils.

- Always supervise pets and children.

- If hamsters get too cold, they may go into hibernation and appear dead. Cup your hamster gently in your hands to warm it up.

Pet words

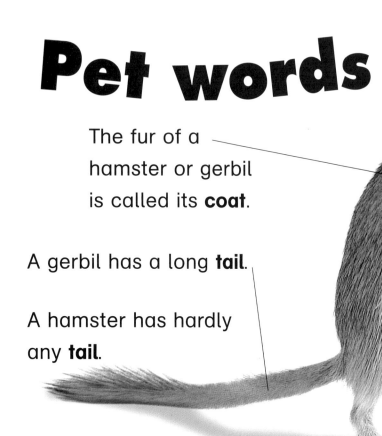

The fur of a hamster or gerbil is called its **coat**.

A gerbil has a long **tail**.

A hamster has hardly any **tail**.

The long hairs on the face of a hamster or gerbil are called **whiskers**.

Hamsters and gerbils have **claws** on their toes.

A **breed** is a special type of hamster or gerbil, such as a Black Mongolian gerbil or Black Syrian hamster.

Index

arrival of pet 14–15
babies 23
bed 12
breeds 6–7
buying pet 8–9
cage 10, 12–13, 20–21
checklists 30–31
claws 17, 32
chew block 18, 19
cleaning 20–21
coat 32
company for pets 8–9

death 28–29
food 11, 18–19
food bowls 11, 21
handling 4, 15, 16–17
hibernation 31
illness 17, 28
ladders 14
life cycle 22–23
life span 5
nest 12
nocturnal animals 4, 5
noise 13, 14

play 5, 16, 24–25
playground 25, 26–27
squealing 17
suckling 23
tail 32
tank 10, 12–13, 20–21
teeth 19
toys 11, 21, 24–25, 31
treats 15, 18
water bottles 11, 19, 21
whiskers 32
wood shavings 10, 20